TEACHER

Bible Readers Series

A Study of James

Putting Faith to Work

Steven Tuell

Abingdon Press / Nashville

Putting Faith to Work
A Study of James

This book is printed on acid-fre1e, elemental chlorine-free paper.

ISBN 0-687-09567-0

04 05 06 07 08 09 10—10 9 8 7 6 5 4
Manufactured in the United States of America.

Contents

James: The Man and the Book

By Steven Tuell

The Book of James is traditionally attributed to James the brother of Jesus, who is mentioned in both lists of Jesus' brothers (Matthew 13:55 and Mark 6:3). During Jesus' lifetime, James apparently did not follow his brother. John 7:5 says that none of Jesus' brothers believed in him. Indeed, in Mark 3:21 we are told that Jesus' family, believing that Jesus was insane, tried to restrain him![1] Jesus, for his part, turned from his family to his followers. Mark 3:31-35 (compare Matthew 12:46-50) describes a painful scene. When Jesus is told that his mother and brothers are looking for him, he asks, "Who are my mother and my brothers?" Then, turning to the crowd, Jesus says, "Here are my mother and my brothers! Whoever does the will of God is my brother and sister and mother" (Mark 3:34-35). Certainly, James would have been deeply hurt and angered by what he must have seen as Jesus' rejection of those closest to him. Still, despite his failure to follow Jesus while Jesus was still alive, James was among the believers waiting for the outpouring of the Spirit at Pentecost (Acts 1:14). Perhaps the reason for this change of heart can be found in 1 Corinthians 15:7, where James is listed among those who had seen the risen Jesus.

After this, James quickly became a leader among the Jewish Christians in Jerusalem. Paul says that, on his first visit to Jerusalem, the only leaders of the church with whom he met were Cephas (the Aramaic form of the name *Peter*) and "James the Lord's brother" (Galatians 1:19). Paul mentions James together with Cephas and John as the "acknowledged pillars" of the Jerusalem church (Galatians 2:9). So, as in Acts 12:17, Peter directs that word of his miraculous deliverance from prison should be taken "to James and to the believers," suggesting that James was the leader of the Jerusalem church. During Paul's final visit to Jerusalem, James and the elders of the Jerusalem church suggested that Paul take a Nazirite vow in order to prove his faithfulness to the law and so make peace with Jews who were hostile toward the church (Acts 21:18-26; for the particulars of the Nazirite vow, see Numbers 6:1-21). Unfortunately, the rumor spread that the people with whom Paul was taking the vow were Gentiles; their presence in the Temple court would have defiled the sanctuary. Rather than making peace with the Jews, as James had hoped, Paul's vow became the cause of Paul's final imprisonment.

We know little about James's personal life. From Paul's statement in 1 Corinthians 9:5, it would appear that James was married; but we know nothing of his wife or children. According to the Jewish historian Josephus, James died at the order of the high priest Ananus, who sentenced him to death by stoning in A.D. 62. The early Christian historian Hegessipus agrees that James was killed by stoning but places his death somewhat later, during the reign of emperor Vespasian, around A.D. 66. Either way, James the brother of Jesus died not long before the Jerusalem Temple was destroyed by the Roman legions in A.D. 70.

THE APOSTOLIC COUNCIL

According to Acts 15, James played the deciding role in the first Apostolic Council, which was called to determine whether Gentiles could be included in the fellowship of believers. While Peter and Paul argued that Gentiles had indeed been called by God, many Jewish Christians remained uncertain. Apparently, of particular concern was the fear that the Gentiles would be immoral. So James announced a compromise. The

Gentile believers were to be recognized as legitimate Christians. However, they also were expected to follow a bare minimum of Jewish law. A letter was written (Acts 15:23-29), calling upon the Gentile believers to "abstain from what has been sacrificed to idols and from blood and from what has been strangled and from fornication" (Acts 15:29).

The legal requirements that James urged upon the new Gentile converts involved the preservation of several essential Jewish ideas. The prohibition against eating food offered to idols meant avoiding even the appearance of idolatry, in keeping with the Jewish idea of monotheism (Exodus 20:1-6). Abstaining from blood is a central principle in Jewish laws of ritual purity, which hold that as the life is in the blood, blood belongs to God alone and cannot be used by humans (Leviticus 17:10-16). Therefore, still today, Jewish law requires that in order for the meat of an animal to be *kosher* (that is, permissible), the animal must be slaughtered in such a way that the blood can be entirely drained from the carcass. The meat of strangled animals is unclean because the blood remains in the meat (Acts 15:29). Finally, requiring that the Gentile Christians abstain from fornication meant holding these new believers to Jewish standards of sexual morality. This would have been particularly important to the Jewish Christians, who apparently considered the Greeks and Romans sexually promiscuous and perverse (Romans 1:24-32).

CONFLICT BETWEEN JAMES AND PAUL

While Acts emphasizes the agreement between Paul and James, Paul's own letters reveal that a considerable gap remained. In Galatians 2 we see the Apostolic Council from Paul's perspective. Paul emphasizes the inclusion of the Gentiles and rejects any legal requirements that would restrict their inclusion. Indeed, Paul describes how he publicly rebuked Peter for snubbing the Gentiles in Antioch (Galatians 2:11-14). Paul attributes Peter's change of heart to "certain people" who "came from James" (Galatians 2:12). These people, called the "circumcision faction" by Paul, are the opponents against whom the arguments in Galatians are addressed.

While Paul certainly agreed that believers must live moral lives, he saw such morality as the *result* of justification, not as an additional requirement. Therefore, Paul contrasts the "works of the flesh" (Galatians 5:16-21) with the "fruit of the Spirit" (Galatians 5:22-26). Paul rejected the idea that anything could be added to the free gift of God, received through faith in Christ: "I do not nullify the grace of God; for if justification comes through the law, then Christ died for nothing" (Galatians 2:21).

Hence, Paul did not consider it necessary for his Gentile converts to regard themselves as bound by even a bare minimum of the Jewish ritual laws of purity. Indeed, Paul feared that insisting upon adherence to such laws could lead to the misunderstanding that we are justified by what we do rather than by God's grace through faith. Therefore, Paul warned that "all who rely upon the works of the law are under a curse" (Galatians 3:10). Legal righteousness before God is impossible; we will always fail at some point and so fall under the curse called down upon those who do not obey the law at *every* point (Galatians 3:10; see also Deuteronomy 27:26; 28:58). Only through faith in the cross of Christ is the curse removed (Galatians 3:13-14).

The eating of food offered to idols is a special case. Unlike James, who seems to have made abstaining from such food an essential requirement for believers, Paul left this matter open. We need to realize that food that had been offered to idols was routinely sold on the open market in the ancient world. Making sure that one abstained from such meat, then, would have meant shopping very carefully. To make absolutely sure one did not eat such food, dinner invitations would have to be avoided. Complicating the picture still more, many trade guilds were dedicated to patron gods or goddesses. Persons determined to avoid eating food offered to idols could not go to the meetings of their guild and as a result could be kept from practicing their profession. In short, this apparently simple prohibition was far more complex and far-reaching in its effects than it appears.

For Paul, no convincing theological reason could be given for avoiding food offered to idols; after all, the gods and goddesses were not true powers in the universe—only the Lord is God. Rather, Paul believed this question to be a matter of pastoral sensitivity. Weaker believers, still young in the faith, may well be tempted to worship idols. Such persons, seeing a stronger Christian knowingly eating food offered to an idol, might fall back into idolatry. "Therefore," Paul said, "if food is the cause of their falling, I will never eat meat, so that I may not cause one of them to fall" (1 Corinthians 8:13).

Paul and James represent two different ways of approaching the gospel in the earliest church. James, it seems, continued to hold for a basically Jewish Christianity, grounded in the essential principles of Jewish ethical and religious law. Paul, however, emphasized justification through faith alone. While he himself remained a Jew, he did not believe it necessary for his Gentile converts to become Jews in order to be Christians. Notice, however, that James and Paul alike would agree that a right relationship with God is ultimately God's gift, that this gift is given through the life and death of Jesus, and that the one who has found life through Christ will practice a moral lifestyle.

THE BOOK OF JAMES

The writer of the Book of James identifies himself simply as "James, a servant of God and of the Lord Jesus Christ" (James 1:1). However, the content of the book, with its emphasis on works of righteousness and its positive attitude toward the law, makes it likely that James the brother of Jesus is intended. The book is addressed to "the twelve tribes in the Dispersion" (James 1:1), which may well indicate a Jewish-Christian audience. Remember, as we observed above, that James was the leader of the Jewish-Christian church in Jerusalem and was very concerned with maintaining the high ethical standards of Judaism. The considerable friction between James and Paul on this point seems to be reflected in the Book of James. Indeed, it seems quite probable that the discussion of faith and works found in James 2:14-26 represents a deliberate response to Paul—especially since Paul's favorite illustration (Abraham) and proof text (Genesis 15:6) are here used to demonstrate a point just the opposite of Paul's: that justification comes by *works,* not faith (compare Romans 4:1-12 and Galatians 3:6-9).

On the other hand, numerous aspects of the Book of James argue against simply assigning the book as a whole to James the brother of Jesus. The book is written in excellent Greek. It uses the vocabulary of a highly educated person; for instance, the technical astronomical language of James 1:17 and the title "Father of lights" are also found in the writings of the Jewish philosopher Philo of Alexandria in Egypt. It is unlikely that James the brother of Jesus would have written in this way.

Because the Book of James deals broadly with universal situations, it is difficult to date precisely. But the book was first accepted as Scripture by the church of Alexandria in Egypt in the third century A.D. and was not accepted by Christians in the West until the fourth century. This could suggest that the book was written late, perhaps in Alexandria. The close parallels between the Book of James and the letters of Paul noted above could mean that the writer had access to the collected writings of Paul, which were not circulated widely until the end of the first century—long after the death of James the brother of Jesus. Similarly, as will be noted in the lessons in this publication, the writer of James appears to have made use of the Gospel of Matthew, especially the Sermon on the Mount (compare James 1:2, 12 with Matthew 5:11-12; James 1:22-23 with Matthew 7:24, 26; James 5:2-3 with Matthew 6:19-21). Since Matthew was probably written between A.D. 80 and A.D. 90, this would once again mean that the book must have been completed after James's death. Finally, many scholars have observed parallels between James and First Peter (for instance, compare James 1:1 to 1 Peter 1:1), as well as such extra-biblical books as First Clement and the Shepherd of Hermas. As these other Christian works come from Rome in the late first to mid-second centuries, the argument is that James as well should be placed in that time.

On the other hand, the literary form of the Book of James suggests a way for us to see the book as both late in its final form and yet still connected to the tradition of James the brother of Jesus. As Lesson 1 in this publication in particular will demonstrate, the "Letter" of James is really not a letter at all. Instead, James appears to be a collection of wise sayings, much like the Book of Proverbs in the Hebrew Bible. A quick look through Proverbs will reveal that, while the book is traditionally associated with the name of Solomon (Proverbs 1:1), Proverbs is in fact a collection of collections, drawn from a variety of people and places (for instance, Proverbs 25:1; 30:1; 31:1). In a similar way, James represents a tradition of Christian wisdom, perhaps stretching over a number of years and through many hands. The final form of the book may well represent only the end point of a long history. I would suggest that the highly ethical, Jewish-Christian traditions we find in the Book of James go back ultimately to James the brother of Jesus, leader of the Jewish Christian church of Jerusalem in the middle of the first century.

[1] Although many translations, including the NRSV, attribute this statement to others present with Jesus, the simplest way to read the Greek text is that it was Jesus' family who said, "He has gone out of his mind."

*Adapted from *Adult Bible Studies Teacher,* June-July-August, 1996 (Copyright © 1996 by Cokesbury).

Chapter One

The Challenge of Hard Times

PURPOSE

To remind us that faith grows out of trials endured, temptations overcome, and beliefs practiced

BIBLE PASSAGE

James 1:2-4, 12-15, 19-27
Background: James 1

CORE VERSES
The testing of your faith produces endurance; and let endurance have its full effect, so that you may be mature and complete, lacking in nothing.
(James 1:3-4)

GET READY

■ During this study, we will be working our way through the Book of James, a book of practical religion. It forces us to accept the fact that the faith we confess has consequences for the life we lead.

You and your class may feel woefully inadequate in light of James's high standards. Remember, however, that James is not the whole gospel. Sometimes we need to hear James's stern warning to "be doers of the word, and not merely hearers who deceive themselves" (James 1:22). At other times we need the reassurance that, when we fail, God is there to forgive us and to empower us to try again. As you work through these five lessons, pray for sensitivity to your class members so that you may help meet their spiritual needs.

BIBLE BACKGROUND

■ Although we speak of the "Letter of James," the book is only superficially in the form of a letter. Comparing James with Paul's short letter to Philemon illustrates the differences. Paul's letter opens with a greeting, identifying Paul as the sender and the church in Philemon's house as the recipient (verses 1-2). Then, following a word of blessing (verse 3), Paul moves on to a thanksgiving for Philemon (verses 4-7). Next comes the body of the letter, expressing Paul's purpose in writing (verses 8-22). Finally, Paul offers greetings from others to Philemon (verses 23-24) and closes with a benediction (verse 25). Apart from a few Christian modifications, this was the way people of Paul's day wrote letters in the Greco-Roman world.

Now compare Philemon to the way James is written. Although James opens like a letter, with a typical greeting (James 1:1), the writer then forgets all about the letter form. In fact, it may seem as though the writer forgets all about any kind of form or structure. Rather than advancing a logically developed and clearly presented argument, James presents short, pithy sayings, loosely arranged by subject. Transitions between sections are abrupt, and the connections are not always clear. For instance, the only apparent connection between James 1:4, on the subject of maturity, and James 1:5, on wisdom, is the word *lacking*. This method of writing, called organization by catch-word, is found especially in the Old Testament Book of Proverbs—another loose collection of short, practical sayings.

In content as well as in form, James resembles Proverbs more than it does anything else in Scripture. Proverbs is a book of ancient Israelite wisdom, teaching the reader how to live rightly before God and others.

We could think of James as a book of early Christian wisdom, aiming—like Proverbs—to teach the reader how to live rightly and well. The major themes of this book are set forth in the first chapter: testing (James 1:2-4, 12-16), wisdom (1:5-8), wealth and the wealthy (1:9-11), good works (1:19-25), and the control of the tongue (1:26-27). These essential ideas are then picked up and developed later in the book.

As we will see especially in Chapter 3, the person responsible for this collection of wise sayings appears to know and respond to the letters of Paul. To be sure, Paul had a profound effect on early Christian writing as well as thought. Of the twenty-seven books in the New Testament, all but six are either actual letters or, like James, books written in the form of letters. Perhaps, then, the reason for the superficial letter form in James is that, at the time this book was written, the letter had become the dominant form of Christian literature.

James 1:1. This is the only part of the Book of James that fits the letter form, and it contains the only mention of James as the writer ***(For more on the identity of this James, see the article "James: The Man and the Book" [pages 5–7 in this publication].).*** This is also one of only two places in the book that mention Jesus Christ (The other is James 2:1.). For this reason and because of the book's focus on works rather than faith, the great Reformer Martin Luther said of James, "I therefore refuse him a place among the writers of the true canon of my Bible."[1]

To be sure, James is not the whole gospel. Our picture of God's plan would be incomplete if we read only James. James does speak to a very important—and often ignored—part of the gospel, however. We can illustrate this with an analogy used, in a different context, by James: the rudder of a ship (3:4). Clearly, the rudder alone cannot make the ship go; for that you need wind for the sails (or fuel for the motors). Yet you must have the rudder to steer. In the same way, the teachings about right living in the Book of James are not enough to motivate and empower a Christian life. For that we need the grace of God, faith in Jesus Christ, and the wind of the Spirit in our sails. However, if we want to steer a clear course through life, putting faith into practice, the wise sayings of James will help us.

James is addressed to "the twelve tribes in the Dispersion" (1:1). Usually, the term *Dispersion* referred to Jews living outside Palestine. However, James is "a servant [the Greek term means literally "slave"] of God and of the Lord Jesus Christ" (1:1). This is a Christian book, addressed to a Christian audience. Probably, then, "the Dispersion" here means the church throughout the world, understood as the new Israel (compare 1 Peter 1:1). Remember, too, that the James whose tradition is continued in this book was a leader of the Jewish Christians in Jerusalem (Acts 12:17; 15:13-21; 21:18; Galatians 2:9, 12). So this book, like the Book of Hebrews, is probably addressed in particular to Jewish Christians.

Verses 2-4. The Book of James opens with advice to consider trials "nothing but joy" (1:2). These words sound quite similar to the words of Jesus in the Sermon on the Mount: "Blessed are you when people revile you and persecute you and utter all kinds of evil against you falsely on my account. Rejoice and be glad, for your reward is great in heaven, for in the same way they persecuted the prophets who were before you" (Matthew 5:11-12). True, as the student book observes, the trials of which James speaks are not persecutions but rather "the ordinary troubles of everyday life" [page 6]. But such troubles and trials can grind us down, wear us out, and rob our lives of joy. Just as Jesus calls those who are reviled and persecuted "happy" (the literal meaning of the Greek word translated "blessed" in both Matthew 5:11 and James 1:12), so James insists that "trials of any kind" can be a source of joy (1:2).

The reason for this affirmation is given in the following two verses. Just as strenuous exercise builds physical endurance, to the end that our bodies become strong and healthy, so spiritual testing produces endurance, leading to spiritual maturity. Notice, however, that this growth is not automatic. The pastor quoted in the section of the student book entitled "Our Need" observed that "most of the people who tell me they have lost their faith say the pain and suffering in their lives is the reason they've turned away from God" [page 5]. Clearly, not everyone grows through trial; some people become bitter or even lose their faith entirely.

Unlike the case with physical exercise, we often have no say in the trials that life brings upon us. No one asks for cancer or an unfaithful spouse or the death of a loved one. Nor do we have any guarantee that trials will come one at a time, in neat order. In fact, it often feels as though everything that can go wrong piles up on us all at once.

Still, we can have a say in how we respond to trials. By practicing the spiritual disciplines of prayer, Bible reading, and public worship, we can build up a store of spiritual strength for our times of trial. Remember, too, that we are not expected to face our trials alone. Just as we should not attempt any exercise regimen without the guidance of a physician, we should not attempt to face the trials of life without the support of Christ's church. As the student book observes, the Book of James presupposes that the reader is part of a Christian community (2:2-3; 5:13-16). With the support and prayers of Christian brothers and sisters and the guidance of spiritual leaders, we can win through trials and become "mature and complete, lacking in nothing" (1:4).

Verses 12-18. Sometimes James's teaching about spiritual growth through suffering leads to the mistaken conclusion that God sends suffering and trials to make us grow. James firmly rejects this idea: "No one, when tempted, should say, 'I am being tempted by God'; for God cannot be tempted by evil and he himself tempts no one" (1:13; note that the Greek word translated "tempted" here is a verbal form of the word translated "trials" in verse 2). This statement is further strengthened by a warning not to be deceived (1:16).

For James the goodness of God means that God cannot be involved with evil, even indirectly. How could "the Father of lights, with whom there is no variation or shadow due to change" (1:17) possibly become a source of darkness? Rather, James insists that God is the source of "every perfect gift" (1:17), to the end that we might "become a kind of first fruits of his creatures" (1:18). God's only involvement in temptation is empowering us to triumph over it so that, having "stood the test," we might "receive the crown of life that the Lord has promised to those who love him" (1:12).

At first, this issue may seem unimportant. What is the difference, after all, between saying that testing leads to spiritual growth, which God certainly wants for us, and saying that God sends trials and temptations in order to make us grow? A moment's thought, however, will show that while the first statement is a spiritual truth, the second is a falsehood. Consider the case of Lee [pages 7–8 in the student book]. We rejoice that, through his illness and suffering, Lee found reconciliation with God and with his family. But suppose I told you that someone had deliberately injected him with the AIDS virus in order to bring these events about? The very idea is monstrous, horrible! Yet is this not the very thing we accuse God of doing if we say that God sent this trial? I believe that good can come out of evil; I cannot believe that God sends evil in order to bring about good.

Those who claim that God is responsible for sending trial and temptation picture God as aloof and above the world, moving us about like pawns on a chess board. However, the entire witness of Scripture and Christian tradition denies that God is anything like this. God is passionately involved with this world—indeed, so involved that God entered the world in the life of Jesus Christ to share our joys, our sorrows, our suffering, and even our death. How can we think that God who loves us so much would try to tempt us to evil?

James insists that blaming temptation upon God denies our responsibility for our own spiritual welfare. Notice the intriguing parallel between verses 3-4 and 14-15. Just as testing leads to endurance and endurance leads to maturity and wholeness, so yielding to desire leads to sin; and sin, to use James's striking image, "gives birth to death" (1:15).

Verses 19-27. The sayings in this section all deal with the relationship between words and actions—beginning, intriguingly, with a reminder not to talk too much (1:19). In these days of TV talk shows and talk radio, we seem to have flipped James's words on their head: Everyone on the airwaves seems quick to speak, quick to anger, and unwilling to listen at all. Far from "clearing the air," such irresponsible and insensitive blather fouls the air, inhibiting the very free speech it claims to represent. The result is much as James warns: "sordidness and rank growth of wickedness" (1:21). No wonder James sternly declares, "If any think they are religious, and do not bridle their tongues but deceive their hearts, their religion is worthless" (1:26).

What is needed, James argues, is not more human words but "the implanted word that has the power to save your souls" (1:21)—the word of God. This divine word must be received in humility and meekness. With Paul, James affirms that our salvation is not a personal accomplishment but a gift of God's grace (Romans 3:23-24.). However, James emphasizes the consequences of welcoming that "implanted word" into our hearts. The life of the believer will be changed—must be changed. The "sordidness and rank growth of wickedness," the anger and self-seeking that for James are the cause of sin and violence, must be rooted out of our lives (James 1:19-21). In short, the word of God cannot remain dormant within us. It must be put into action (1:22).

We will return to this question of faith and works later in this study. For now, note that James and Paul do not proclaim a different gospel but rather the same gospel with different points of emphasis.

In these verses we again find an intriguing parallel between James and the Sermon on the Mount. Remember that, at the close of that message, Jesus tells the story of the wise builder, who built on the rock, and the foolish builder, who built on sand (Matthew 7:24-27). The house built on the rock could stand against rain, wind, and flood; but the house with no foundation was swept away. The point of the story is found in Matthew 7:24 and 26. The wise builder, Jesus says, stands for everyone "who hears these words of mine and acts on them"; the foolish builder stands for "everyone who hears these words of mine and does not act on them." For Jesus as for James, it is clear that hearing the word is not enough. The word must be put into practice in the way we live our lives. James rejects casual Christianity, comparing those who hear the word but do not act upon it to people glancing in a mirror, then looking away and immediately forgetting what they saw (James 1:23-24). The word of God holds a mirror up to our lives, showing us ourselves as we truly are. We cannot afford to treat that revelation casually. If we do not conform our lives to the implanted word within, we deceive ourselves; and our "faith" is no faith at all.

James describes the word of God as law, which may be a surprise. We are accustomed to thinking of the law in negative terms, as a bondage from which the gospel of Christ has set us free. James, however, speaks of the gospel as "the perfect law, the law of liberty" (1:25). The gospel is law, inasmuch as it places a demand upon us. As James everywhere makes clear, Christians are not "free" to behave as they like, yielding to their own selfish desires, refusing to listen to others or to learn from their own mistakes—not if they want to remain Christians. However, the word of God is the perfect law of wholeness and completion. The gospel is what makes it possible for us to reach the goal set out in James 1:4: "that you may be mature and complete, lacking in nothing."

Further, the word of God is the law of freedom. Those who live moment to moment without discipline or direction may think that they are free; but, in fact, they are caught up in the cruelest bondage of all. They are slaves to their own selfish desires, unable even to think of resisting temptation. The obligations of the gospel, then, which place us under obedience to Christ, set us free from bondage to sin and self. James, the self-described slave of Christ, is freer than anyone.

INTRODUCE OUR NEED

■ Recently, I went to the funeral of a friend—a young mother with two children, a loving husband, and everything in the world to live for. I listened to a well-meaning family friend saying that we should not grieve, that my friend was with Jesus and the angels. As I listened, I became more and more angry. Why shouldn't we grieve? Why shouldn't we rage against the injustice of this life so tragically and unfairly cut short?

When the pastor began to speak, it was a relief to hear him begin by saying, "This day is an abomination before God. Children shouldn't die before their parents. Little girls shouldn't lose their mother. A husband shouldn't be robbed of his best friend and soul mate." The pastor went on to speak of the Resurrection, of new life, of the power and presence of God. But I was comforted first of all by having my grief and the grief of the family acknowledged and affirmed.

James reminds us that we can grow through suffering and trial, that good can come from evil. I know that my friend's life reflected joy and confidence in the presence of God, a confidence hard-worn and proven through suffering and trial. I know that my life is better for having known this woman. I know too that through her long struggle against cancer, her doctors learned much about her disease that can be used to treat others so that some other child may not have to weep at a mother's funeral. But I will not believe that God gave my friend cancer in order to teach her or me or anyone else a lesson. James, who speaks of the hard lessons learned from trials, also rejects the idea that God is the author of temptation and testing. It would be a shame if, having learned the first lesson from James, we failed to learn the other.

LESSON PLAN

■ Following your opening prayer, ask: ***How do we go about writing a letter?*** (*If people are slow to respond, prompt them with questions such as, "What comes first?" and "What would you write next?" As people suggest parts of a letter, write them down on a chalkboard or on a large piece of paper. Probably, your letter will begin with "Dear So-and-so," then move on to something like "How are you? I am fine." before getting down to the body of the letter. Then the letter will probably close with "Sincerely" or "Yours truly," followed by the signature. Tell your class that letter writing in the first century also followed a clear structure [You may want to use Philemon as an example.].*)

Now turn to the "letter" of James. Note that, while the text begins like a letter, it has none of the other features we would expect to find in a letter. Describe for your class the similarities in structure and content between Proverbs and James noted above, suggesting that James is an example of early Christian wisdom literature.

You may also want to discuss the authorship of James, using the article on pages 5–7 in this publication. Note, at any rate, that the book is addressed to "the twelve tribes in the Dispersion," which could suggest a Jewish Christian audience in keeping with the traditions associated with James, the brother of Jesus and leader of the Jerusalem church.

Now turn to the text of James. Ask someone to read aloud James 1:2-4. Then ask the question at the end of the introduction to the student book section entitled "Faithful Living" [page 9]: ***"What experiences have you had of times of hardship that were also times of joy?"*** (*If the class members are slow to answer, break the ice with a story of your own or with the story of Lee in the student book or with the story of the young mother with cancer above. Some class members may mention times of illness or joblessness or loneliness when they found God very close to them. Others may question whether hardship can ever really be a joy.*)

Recall the pastor's words about loss of faith during times of trial found above and in the student book: Then ask: ***How do we live as people of faith in the midst of the trials of life?*** (*A variety of answers are possible: by having a strong, positive self-image as a person loved by God; by receiving the support of Christian friends; by praying; by Bible reading; and so forth.*)

Remind your class that James is a Christian text and presupposes that the reader is involved in a Christian community. Note that he addresses his readers as "brothers and sisters," assumes that they are part of an assembly (2:1-4), and speaks of "the elders of the church" (5:14). Our fellowship as the body of Christ is meant to be a source of strength and support.

Now ask: ***Does God send trials? Why or why not?*** (*Some class members may want to claim that God does send trials in order to make us strong. Note, however, that James rejects this way of thinking about God [James 1:13].*) James insists that we are responsible for our own spiritual welfare. Temptations do not come from God but rather from our own uncontrolled desires. We could say that, for James, it is the "me-first" attitude that lies behind all human sin. You may want to review the discussion from above or refer to the illustration from the "Introduce Our Need" section.

Move next to the final section of this lesson in the student book, entitled "Shaping Words and Actions," by reading aloud James 1:19-21, 26. We sometimes chant the little rhyme "Sticks and stones may break my bones, but words will never hurt me." However, we all know that is a lie. Words can bring great pain and do untold damage. In contrast to the destructive power of human words, James affirms the creative power of God's implanted word. As the student book observes, to speak of the "implanted word" is to affirm, with Jeremiah 31:33b, that God's word has become a part of us. This cannot help but make a difference in our conduct. James therefore affirms that we must put that word into action: "Religion that is pure and undefiled before God, the Father, is this: to care for orphans and widows in their distress, and to keep oneself unstained by the world" (James 1:27).

Ask a class member to read aloud James 1:22. Then ask the question at the end of the lesson in the student book [page 12]: ***"How through your words and through your care for those in need can you be a more faithful doer of the word of God?"*** (*Class members may suggest visiting shut-ins or volunteering in one of the ministries of your church. Some may also want to resolve to speak well of others and to avoid idle gossip that can wound others.*)

After all who wish to do so have responded, lift your resolutions to God in prayer. Then close the session by having the class sing "Lord, I Want to Be a Christian."

[1] From Luther's "Preface to the Epistles of St. James and St. Jude," in *Martin Luther: Selections From His Writings*, edited and with an introduction by John Dillenberger (Doubleday & Company, Inc., 1961); page 36.

TRY ANOTHER METHOD

■ Since the overall theme of this lesson is Christian growth, particularly through trials, you may want to use ten or fifteen minutes of this session for a personal testimony from someone in your church, in your community, or perhaps even in your class who has experienced growth through trial and hardship. Almost certainly, you know someone who would be willing to share her or his experience of God's faithfulness in trying times. Such a testimony would add particular force to James's advice that we consider our trials "nothing but joy" (James 1:2).

Chapter Two

LOVE IMPARTIALLY

PURPOSE

To challenge us to live with integrity in our relationships with all people

BIBLE PASSAGE

James 2:1-13; 4:11-12

CORE VERSE
You do well if you really fulfill the royal law according to the scripture, "You shall love your neighbor as yourself." (James 2:8)

GET READY

■ Not many of us think of ourselves as wealthy people. However, by the standards of most of the world, most of us are rich indeed. Few of us need to worry about food or shelter or clothing. This places us among the world's rich—making it hard to read such passages as, "The rich will disappear like a flower in the field" (James 1:10) or, "Has not God chosen the poor in the world to be rich in faith and to be heirs of the kingdom that he has promised to those who love him?" (James 2:5).

The major issue in these texts, however, is not the attitude that we have toward wealth but the attitude we have toward one another. As you prepare for this lesson, pray for the poor in your community. Think about ways that you and your class can be used of God to minister to those most in need.

BIBLE BACKGROUND

■ **James 2:1-4.** Our text begins with a challenge: "My brothers and sisters, do you with your acts of favoritism really believe in our glorious Lord Jesus Christ?" (2:1). James's implied answer to his own question is, "No." Showing favoritism is not merely an error of judgment but a violation of the essential character of the faith. The proof of faith is a life of love—an idea found throughout the New Testament. In 1 John 4:20, we read, "Those who say, 'I love God,' and hate their brothers or sisters are liars." According to Matthew 25:31-46, the principle by which the Son of Man will judge the world is, "Just as you did it to one of the least of those who are members of my family, you did it to me" (Matthew 25:40).

James illustrates his point by describing an incident that could happen in his own community—and one that could happen in our churches as well. Two people come into the assembly. One appears "with gold rings and in fine clothes" (2:2). In the first century, a gold ring was the mark of a senator or a Roman nobleman, indicating that this first person in James's illustration was not only wealthy but also politically powerful. The other who enters the assembly is "a poor person in dirty clothes" (2:2). Now, how will the community respond?

In James's example the church responded by showing honor to the rich person and snubbing the poor person. Sadly, James's illustration probably reflects our experience as well. We are usually more comfortable with "our kind" of people. We welcome folks like us but are uneasy with people from different social backgrounds—specifically, we are uncomfortable with the poor. As a result, our churches often become what sociologists call "homogeneous" communities; that is, they become groups in which everyone is more or less the same as everyone else. In such a community we feel comfortable and safe. Homogeneous churches, therefore, may well also be "successful" churches—judged in terms of growth and financial stability.

James, however, raises a serious and disturbing question: Is the church supposed to be a place where we can have fellowship with our own kind? where we can feel comfortable and safe? Or, is the church intended to be a community reaching out into the world, open to all kinds of people? Remember that Jesus' last charge to the church, according to Matthew's Gospel, was, "Go therefore and make disciples of all nations" (Matthew 28:19). James poses the question in stark terms: If we are not an open, inclusive community, how can we claim to be the church at all? Where is the evidence that we "really believe in our glorious Lord Jesus Christ" (2:1)?

Verses 5-7. For James this favoritism for the rich is bitterly ironic. The people the church is actively courting, James asserts, are the very ones who are its enemies. The rich, he says, oppress the church, dragging its members into the law courts and generally blaspheming "the excellent name that was invoked over you" (2:6-7).

We need to remember that James is not speaking here of the rich in general, any more than James 2:1-4 describes the church in general. Not all churches show partiality, and not all rich persons are guilty of oppression and blasphemy. Indeed, the New Testament speaks of wealthy, politically influential people of faith (for example, Luke 8:3; Acts 8:27; 10:1-2; Philemon).

In the experience of James's community, however, persecution and oppression had generally come from the upper levels of society. As members of the lower classes, James's community would have had plenty of experience with economic oppression; and as Christians, they also would have experienced religious persecution. Since Christians refused to worship idols and would not take part in the cults dedicated to the Roman emperors, they stood out in the various cities and towns where they lived. As a result, Christians were considered an undesirable minority and encountered opposition from the local authorities. Since the rich were also the politically well-connected, they would have been the source of much of the trouble the early church faced (James 5:1-6.). How, James asks, can Christians be so foolish as to show preference for the very people who are trying to destroy them?

Just as James's words about the rich opponents of the church should not be read as condemning all wealthy people, his words about the poor should not be understood to mean that all poor people are virtuous. Far too many charitable enterprises have shipwrecked on a false, romanticized view of the poor. We must never forget that poor people are people first and like all people are capable of love and hate, goodness and evil. We need to ask, then, what James means by "the poor."

Recall first, as we observed above, that for James "the rich" were those wealthy persons involved in oppressing the church economically and religiously. Similarly, "the poor" would have meant, specifically, those persons who belonged to the communities facing oppression. For that reason James could say, "Let the believer who is lowly boast in being raised up, and the rich in being brought low, because the rich will disappear like a flower in the field" (1:9-10). The believer (literally, "the brother" in Greek), who is of course poor and lowly, will be exalted. In contrast, the rich must either be brought low; or else, "in the midst of a busy life, they will wither away" (1:11).

The danger of wealth is that it is a distraction from the truly important tasks of the gospel. "The rich" are those who are occupied with many things—busy, in James's words—and so are kept from wholehearted devotion to the gospel. One is reminded of Jesus saying, "How hard it will be for those who have wealth to enter the kingdom of God!" (Mark 10:23).

However, as the student book observes, "Material possessions can be a stumbling block for the poor as well as for the rich" [page 18]. Anxiety about possessions can eat away at the poor, who worry about having enough, as well as at the rich, who can become obsessed with holding on to what they have. The drug traffic that has become the curse of the inner city thrives because of the temptation of affluence, particularly to those who see no way out of grinding poverty except crime. Perhaps that is why James says, "Religion that is pure and undefiled before God, the Father, is this: . . . to keep oneself unstained by the world" (1:27).

Now we are ready to hear what James is saying in 2:5: "Has not God chosen the poor in the world to be rich in faith and to be heirs of the kingdom that he has promised to those who love him?" Notice that, once again, the language of James sounds very much like the language of the Sermon on the Mount: "Blessed are the poor in spirit, for theirs is the kingdom of heaven" (Matthew 5:3). These many parallels prompted New Testament scholar W.D. Davies to say that "it is in the Epistle of James that the words of Jesus break through more often than in any other document outside the Synoptics."[1] However, as the student book observes, in this case the text of James appears closer to Luke's version of the first beatitude:

> Blessed are you who are poor,
> for yours is the kingdom of God.
> (Luke 6:20)

In Luke's version, as in James, it is simply "the poor" who are promised the Kingdom. Luke seems also to fit the spirit of James by matching this blessing upon the poor with a corresponding curse upon the rich:

> But woe to you who are rich,
> for you have received your consolation.
> (Luke 6:24)

Notice, though, that James also says, God has "chosen the poor in the world to be rich in faith" (2:5). As we have seen, "the poor" in James are the members of the believing community, whose lives are focused, without material distractions, upon the gospel. This emphasis upon spiritual poverty is in keeping with Matthew's "poor in spirit." The point is not simply possessions or the lack of them but whether a life is focused on the gospel or on its own desires.

Verses 8-13. These verses apparently respond to an imagined retort from the assembly James had strongly chastised in the previous verses. "When we treat the rich with respect," they might reply, "we are only obeying the law (Leviticus 19:18), which requires us to show love."

Note first of all that James accepts the argument at face value; that is, he does not respond by denying the legitimacy of the law. James is capable of referring to the gospel as law, though rarely simply as *the* law. Instead, James uses the term *law* with qualifying expressions that describe more fully what "law" means for him. So, in James 1:25, it is "the perfect law, the law of liberty"; in 2:12, "the law of liberty" once more; and here, in 2:8, "the royal law."

One possible interpretation of the last expression is that the law of love stated in Leviticus 19:18 ("You shall love your neighbor as yourself.") is royal because it is the highest of the laws. This concept is central to the teaching of Jesus, who expressed it in the form of the Golden Rule: "In everything do to others as you would have them do to you; for this is the law and the prophets" (Matthew 7:12). In Matthew 22:34-40 (compare Mark 12:28-34 and Luke 10:25-28), Leviticus 19:18 is quoted by Jesus as the second great commandment, the first being Deuteronomy 6:5 ("You shall love the Lord your God with all your heart, and with all your soul, and with all your mind" [Matthew 22:37].). "On these two commandments," Jesus says, "hang all the law and the prophets" (Matthew 22:40). Intriguingly, Leviticus 19:18 is added to the laws cited from the Ten Commandments in Matthew 19:19 as part of Jesus' answer to the rich young man seeking eternal life (compare Mark 10:17-31 and Luke 18:18-30). In these sayings, love is set forth as both the highest law and the essential principle back of the law.

This way of summarizing the law in the principle of love is an idea also found in the teachings of the greatest Jewish rabbis. The story is told of a Gentile who came to the famous rabbi Hillel and asked if the rabbi could tell him the essence of the law while standing on one foot. Balanced on one foot, Hillel replied, "Do not do to others what is hateful to yourself. That is the Torah [Hebrew for *law*]. The rest is commentary." Notice that Hillel's summary of the law is a negative version of Jesus' Golden Rule. Perhaps through his training as a Pharisee, Paul learned this same idea and applied it in his teachings. Twice in his letters Paul quotes Leviticus 19:18, each time as a summary of the entire law (Romans 13:8-9; Galatians 5:14).

Another interpretation of the phrase "royal law" is that this is the law of the Kingdom. Remember that James refers to the poor as "heirs of the kingdom" (2:5). Perhaps both interpretations are intended here. As the highest law and the principle upon which the law is based, the command to love your neighbor is a fitting candidate for the law of Christ's kingdom, which those who inherit the Kingdom will apply.

Now we can return to James's argument. Yes, he says to his imaginary opponent, it is right and proper for you to fulfill the royal law by loving even the rich. However, be sure that that is in fact what you are doing. Because if instead you are using the law to justify "toadying up" to the rich and rejecting the poor, then you are in violation of the law and will be condemned. James argues that breaking the law on only one point is still breaking the whole law. Appeal to the law in a legalistic defense, then, does not get the community off the hook but instead puts them in even deeper trouble.

Fortunately, James reminds us, we do not have to be caught in a legal bind. For the royal law of love is also a law of freedom (2:12). Fulfilling this command in truth by showing love impartially for rich and poor alike will result in our liberation. We are ourselves judged, James says, according to the standards by which we judge others: "For judgment will be without mercy to anyone who has shown no mercy"; but fortunately, "mercy triumphs over judgment" (2:13).

James 4:11-13. This principle of judgment is also expressed in the closing verses of our Bible passage. Here the believer is warned against evil speech and harsh judgments, since the person who so judges another places herself or himself above the law that should provide the community's standard. God alone is able to apply the standards of judgment in the Kingdom. We are free to love without qualification, confident that God will do all the judging that is necessary.

INTRODUCE OUR NEED

■ When I started seminary, I found myself in a new place, surrounded by new people, in a new part of the country. For the first time in my life, I was too far from home to pack up and go there whenever I wanted. Many of the people I met seemed cold and distant. I repeatedly found my attempts to make friends rebuffed. I felt worthless; rejected; and very, very alone.

Because of an unexpectedly large enrollment, I was placed, along with ten or twelve other students, in a decaying, red-brick mansion used for overflow housing. We called the place The Pits Ritz or The Pits for short. There I found a loving, accepting, and decidedly unconventional Christian community.

The guys in the Pits came from a variety of religious backgrounds and from all over the country. We debated theology, studied the Bible together, and bounced our sermons off one another—as well as having indoor snowball fights, sunning on the roof, and challenging all comers to no-holds-barred water battles.

I have often wondered what might have happened to me if I had not been placed in The Pits. Would I have become cold and withdrawn myself? Desperate to be accepted, would I have tried to turn myself into someone else? I thank God for directing me to a place of warmth and acceptance and to people who modeled the impartial love James described.

LESSON PLAN

■ Open the session by praying a prayer that recalls some essential ideas from Chapter One and leads into this lesson. Then ask the question that opens the lesson in the student book [page 14]: ***"What factors bring a person high regard, admiration, and acceptance in our society?"*** (*Likely, the items mentioned in the student book will head the list of the class members' responses.*) Next ask: ***What factors bring a person high regard, admiration, and acceptance in our church?*** (*Some class members will mention faith in Christ, honesty, a moral life, and similar virtues. Others, however, may observe that, in practice, the church is all too often influenced by the same factors that count for high regard in the world. We too are easily drawn to successful, attractive, clean-cut people and repelled by poor, unattractive, unwashed people—even when we think we should not be.*)

Turn now to the first verse of our Bible passage. Note that, for James, showing favoritism is a serious matter. Favoritism is a denial of the principle of love and acceptance that lies at the foundation of the faith and therefore calls our very Christianity into question. To illustrate his point, James presents a situation for consideration. Suppose two people, one well-dressed and obviously powerful, the other dressed poorly and shabbily, entered our assembly. How would we respond? It is sad to realize that probably, in most of our churches, what James describes would likely take place: The rich person would be honored, and the poor person would be rejected.

Write the word "homogeneous" on a chalkboard or on a large piece of paper. Ask for definitions from the class. If no one is able to give the proper definition, you do so and then summarize the discussion above on homogeneous churches. Ask: ***Is the church supposed to be a place where we feel comfortable and safe? Why or why not?*** (*Some class members may well say yes, that they could not worship in a place where they did not feel at home. Others, though, will perhaps observe that in our comfort with one another, we may well shut out others.*) Refer to the church mentioned in the student book that turned African Americans away from the Lord's Table in the 1960's [page 16]. Remind your class that the church is not meant to be a place for us to gather in comfort with our "own kind" but rather a place of outreach and inclusion.

The student book makes reference to those Tex Sample calls "hard living people"—the very kind of people James describes in his illustration. Read the description from the student book [page 17]; then ask: ***Are "hard living people" welcome in our assemblies? Why or why not?*** (*Some class members may well say that these people should feel welcome, that the church is a friendly place. Think, though: Does the church, which feels so comfortable to insiders, feel comfortable to outsiders?*) Invite your class to picture the congregation in your sanctuary Sunday after Sunday. Ask: ***Are there, in fact, any "hard living people" present?***

Have a class member read aloud James 2:5-7. Then

ask: ***How does this text make you feel?*** (*Some members will say that they feel threatened. Some may well ask why James is so hard on the rich and so favorable to the poor. Others may see this as just another example of the church's namby-pamby "rich is bad, poor is good" attitude. Notice, however, that we do need to consider the situation in the early church to understand what is going on here.*)

Summarize the discussion above on the rich. Note that, while the Bible does mention well-to-do people of faith, the early church generally encountered persecution from the local political authorities. These people would have been among the rich. So in James's experience the members of the community of faith would typically be from among the poor. Notice that in James 1:9-11 it is assumed that "the believer" is among the "lowly." However, the rich are not simply condemned but are to be brought low. The assumption appears to be that the busy rich do not have the time to devote to what, finally, matters most of all: the gospel.

Have your class look up the Beatitudes in Matthew 5:3 and Luke 6:20 and compare them to James 2:5. Notice the parallels. Luke, like James, reminds us that God sides with the poor and oppressed and against those who oppress them. Matthew emphasizes spiritual poverty: eliminating distractions and focusing on God and God's will. Perhaps this is what James means when he says that God has "chosen the poor . . . to be rich in faith" (2:5). However, as the student book observes, "Material possessions can be a stumbling block for the poor as well as for the rich" [page 18]. All of us need to learn that faith in Christ and the life of love that follows from faith are ultimately the only things that matter.

James refers to love for the neighbor as "the royal law" (2:8). Summarize for your class the discussion above on the law of love as both the highest of laws and the law of Christ's kingdom. James speaks this way in order to emphasize the importance, the centrality, of impartial love in the church. If we insist on judging others, that is, as to whether they are worthy of our love, we put ourselves in the place of God, the only wise judge (James 4:11-12). Impartial, accepting love is the sure demonstration of belief in Christ. Where there is no love, there is no true faith.

Ask the question at the end of the introduction to the section in the student book entitled "Faithful Living" [page 17]: ***"How can you and your church grow in your ability to see people as Christ sees them and to welcome them as Christ's representatives?"*** (*Some class members may suggest involvement in ministry to the poor through a soup kitchen or clothes pantry. This is a good idea; but note that it is possible still to see the poor as candidates for mission, not membership. Other class members may say that they have invited poor people to church but that these people have not come. Suggest that class members think about ways that your church can be more welcoming. Perhaps your class could volunteer to act as greeters and to help plan and conduct a worship service in which the music and the liturgy are more accessible to people who do not know the hymns of the church or the Lord's Prayer or the Apostles' Creed.*)

Finally, though, it is our attitudes that need changing more than our programs. Lead your class in a prayer of confession, asking God to forgive our partiality and lack of love. An appropriate hymn for closing this session is "Help Us Accept Each Other."

[1] From *The Setting of the Sermon on the Mount*, by W.D. Davies (Cambridge University Press, 1964); page 402.

TRY ANOTHER METHOD

■ The situation described in James 2:1-4 is ideal for roleplay. If there is a clown troupe in your church or in your district, you way want to ask them to come and act out this scene in mime. Or if you have in your class people who are gifted in dramatics, you may want to ask them to put together a presentation of this simple, powerful scene. Be sure to approach your actors well in advance, however, to give them time to prepare.

Chapter 3 Three

LIVING FAITHFULLY

PURPOSE

To affirm that faith and good works are inseparable

BIBLE PASSAGE

James 2:14-26; 5:13-16
Background: James 2:14-26; 5:7-20

CORE VERSE
Just as the body without the spirit is dead, so faith without works is also dead. (James 2:26)

GET READY

■ Our Bible passage includes the famous "faith without works is dead" passage (James 2:14-26)—probably the best-known text from the Book of James. Unfortunately, this is also one of the most misinterpreted texts in Scripture. Read as a justification of "works-righteousness," this text can either bring us to despair over our failures or tempt us into self-righteous smugness.

But that is not the only way to read this text. As you prepare for the session, take care to observe what James and Paul mean by the terms *faith* and *works.* Meditate prayerfully on this passage and on what God is saying to you and to your class through these words.

Before the session, read carefully Genesis 22:1-19 and Joshua 2:1-21; 6:22-25. Also, you may wish to prepare the chart described below in "Lesson Plan" as a poster prior to the session.

BIBLE BACKGROUND

■ Our Bible passage opens with two powerful questions: "What good is it, my brothers and sisters, if you say you have faith but do not have works? Can faith save you?" (James 2:14). The order of these questions is important. Posed alone, the second question would have an entirely different ring. Can faith save us? The answer, of course, is yes; in fact, only faith in Christ can save us.

However, listen to what James is telling us. The first question makes clear exactly what kind of "faith" James has in mind. Faith without works is faith that demands nothing from us and makes no difference in the life of the person who claims it—a "stealth" faith that cannot be detected. Surely such a faith is really no faith at all—which is why James writes, "What good is it . . . if *you* say [italics added] you have faith?" (2:14). Clearly, saying and having are two different things.

James is not setting up a contrast between works and faith. Rather, he is contrasting true faith and false faith. True faith will show itself by works. False faith, stealth faith, makes no difference in our lives or in our world. Little wonder that James asks, "What good is it?"

James 2:15-17. Here, as in James 2:2-3, we are confronted with a situation that could happen anytime, anywhere. Once more we must sadly confess that James's description of the situation is all too accurate. Faced with human need, with hunger, with homelessness, with poverty, we respond far too glibly with expressions of concern, while giving far too little of our resources, our time, or ourselves. James neatly punctures our pretensions, asking, "What is the good of that?" (2:16).

To say as James does that "faith by itself, if it has no

works, is dead" (2:17) is, once more, not to contrast faith with works. James rather asserts that faith that does not show itself by works is not faith at all. Martin Marty writes wryly of a church starting a stewardship campaign with, the church's literature proclaimed, "a refreshing new emphasis." The church's chairperson of the board wrote, "We will not use the word commitment, budget or pledge. People do not join a church to be committed or challenged."[1] James, to the contrary, reminds us that without commitment and challenge, there is no faith.

Verses 18-19. As in verses 8-13, James here sets up a hypothetical situation, building on his previous examples. Suppose someone were to assert that faith and works are two separate realities: Some have faith; others do works. James asks, in effect, "How can we know, then, whether the person who claims to have faith truly does? What is the proof of such a faith?" My wife, Wendy, tells me that she loves me; but she also shows me her love in countless ways. True love cannot be kept secret. It will reveal itself in the way the lover acts toward the beloved. Just so, James says, the proof of faith must be a different kind of life: "I by my works will show you my faith" (2:18).

Now we come to the crux of James's argument. What kind of faith does not reveal itself by works? The only answer James can come up with is an abstract, intellectual faith, better called *belief*: "You *believe* [italics added] that God is one; you do well" (2:19). Indeed, still today, this is what many people mean by faith: the belief that something is true. However, as James makes clear, belief alone is not really faith—at any rate, it is not saving faith with the power to transform lives. Even the demons, after all, believe in God. Remember that in Mark's Gospel the demons are the first to recognize who Jesus is (1:23-24, 32-34). However, no demon ever became a disciple. Clearly then, belief alone is not a sufficient definition of true, saving faith. So what does saving faith mean? To answer this question, James turns to the Scriptures.

Verses 20-26. Once again, James begins his argument with a blunt, pointed question: "Do you want to be shown, you senseless person, that faith apart from works is barren?" (2:20). Note that where, before, James had used the image of death to describe faith that is really no faith, here he uses the image of barrenness. Faith that does not issue forth in good works is barren faith; it produces nothing. On the other hand, true faith will not be barren but will bear fruit in the life of the believer.

Paul uses a similar image in Galatians 5:22-25, where he speaks of the lifestyle of the believer as the "fruit of the Spirit." Jesus makes the same point in the Sermon on the Mount: "Are grapes gathered from thorns, or figs from thistles? In the same way, every good tree bears good fruit, but the bad tree bears bad fruit" (Matthew 7:16-17). As James speaks of "justification by works" in the following verses, note that for him as well as for Paul and Jesus, good works proceed from a life of faith.

It is surely significant that James's first illustration of justification by works is Abraham (2:21-24), Paul's favorite illustration of justification by faith. In Galatians 3:6-9, Paul responds to the legalistic arguments of those Jewish Christians who insist that obedience to Jewish ritual law (including sabbath observance, circumcision, and keeping kosher) is necessary for salvation. He goes back to the ancestor of all the Jews, to Abraham himself, to ask how Abraham was justified in God's sight. For Paul, the answer is clear: As Genesis 15:6 plainly states, Abraham "believed the LORD; and the LORD reckoned it to him as righteousness." If Abraham, the first Jew, was justified before God by his faith, then those who trust in the promises of God as Abraham did are Abraham's true descendants. Later, Paul reminds us that this covenant of faith with Abraham was made long before the law was given to Moses—indeed, long before Moses was even born (Galatians 3:15-18). Therefore, the law cannot set aside the promise God had already established for Abraham and all who, like Abraham, believe in God's promise. Paul states this principle in strong, uncompromising terms: "We know that a person is justified not by the works of the law but through faith in Jesus Christ" (Galatians 2:16).

At first, it appears that James is using the same illustration to make the opposite point. Abraham, James says, was justified by works: specifically, by his willingness to offer his son Isaac up to God (Genesis 22:1-19). Indeed, James asserts that this is the true meaning of Genesis 15:6. Abraham acted upon his belief in God and therefore was reckoned righteous. So James concludes, "You see that a person is justified by works and not by faith alone" (2:24).

Without doubt, James is making a deliberate response to Paul. The use of Paul's vocabulary ("justification"), Paul's favorite illustration, and even the same proof text from Genesis all make it clear that James intends for us to bounce his observations off of Paul's. However, it is not at all clear that James's position is contradictory to Paul's. James and Paul used many of the same words; but they used them in different, not contradictory, ways. As we have seen above, when James uses the word *faith* in this essay, he is not thinking of saving, committed faith. Rather, he speaks of "faith alone" (2:24), of faith that "is barren" (2:20) and "dead" (2:17, 26). Paul would agree that that sort of faith cannot save anybody. When Paul speaks of faith, he means the commitment of the whole person to Christ so that Paul can say, "I have been crucified with Christ" (Galatians 2:19).

Consider too that when Paul speaks of "works" which cannot save, he is not speaking, as James does, of acts demonstrating commitment and love. Rather, as the student book observes [page 28], Paul is referring to works of the law: legalistic adherence to the ritual laws of Judaism. Paul's point is that nothing can be added to the free, gracious gift of God in Jesus Christ.

Paul would insist that faith has definite consequences for the life of the believer, however. Throughout his ministry Paul struggled against a serious misinterpretation of his gospel: the claim that since our justification is God's free gift offered through the crucifixion of God's Son, Jesus, we can live as we please. Paul denies that this is the case. The believer, he affirms, has died to sin and to the world (Romans 6:1-4) and has been born into a new life, lived under the direction of God's Spirit (Romans 8:1-17). This is what James is getting at as well when he describes faith as "active along with . . . works" and as being "brought to completion by the works" (2:22).

James's second illustration, Rahab the prostitute, confirms this association (Her story is found in Joshua 2:1-21; 6:22-25.). Rahab believed in God; she said to the Israelite spies, "The LORD your God is indeed God in heaven above and on earth below" (Joshua 2:11). More importantly, however, she had faith in God. Acting upon her belief, she risked her life by concealing the spies and helping them escape from Jericho. Her faith too was shown to be active and alive by her works.

As the student book puts it, "Both Paul and James see good works as necessary to genuine religion and as an expression of faith in the God revealed in Jesus Christ" [pages 28–29]. Their difference lies in their emphases. Paul places the accent on the grace of God, received through faith. James emphasizes our human response and the nature of our lives lived under God's grace.

James 5:13-16. From general teachings about the nature of faith, we move now to practical application in the life of a worshiping community. These verses remind us, first of all, that the Book of James is Christian wisdom, to be read and applied in the context of a community of faith. In that community context, private suffering is shared in prayer; and private joy is lifted up in communal songs of praise. In this way, the need of one becomes the need of all; and the joy of one becomes the joy of all. James expresses, finally, the confidence that even sickness should not sever the bonds of community. Rather, the sick person should be ministered to by the community through its leaders, the elders.

As we have already seen, for James the only real faith is faith in action. Little wonder, then, that he here affirms confidently the power of the prayer of faith to bring about healing and forgiveness of sins—healing, that is, of body and of spirit. All too often, however, the very definite, positive language of James 5:13-16 ("The prayer of faith will save the sick.") has been misused to transform prayer for healing into a magical rite. Some say, "If you pray in the name of Jesus, in faith believing, you will get whatever you ask for." Such an attitude is harmful to the sick, to their friends, and to their families; for it subjects them needlessly to guilt and anxiety: "If I had only prayed hard enough, if my faith had only been strong enough, my loved one would have been healed." It is but a short step from this attitude to blaming the victim for her or his illness. Worst of all, by thinking to command God, such an approach is idolatrous in the extreme.

Without question we should pray for the sick. Without question when we pray, we should believe that God hears and answers prayer; otherwise, there would be little point in praying. However, we must never forget who is the worshiper and who is the Worshiped.

James 5:7-12, not printed in the student book, serves as a needed brake on the unrestrained, uncritical use of James 5:13-16. With its teaching of patient endurance in the face of suffering, James 5:7-12 recalls James 1:2-4 on growth through trial. The believer cannot, through the prayer of faith, simply banish adversity. Only at the end, when the Lord returns, will all suffering and pain be abolished. In the meantime the believer is to follow the example of the prophets, who were faithful even when ignored, and of Job, whose endurance proved the compassion of God (James 5:10-11).

INTRODUCE OUR NEED

■ When I was in full-time parish ministry, I once suggested to my churches that we spend Sunday evenings in Bible study rather than in a second preaching service. My idea was voted down by the administrative council, which was a disappointment but not a surprise. I *was* surprised, though, when one of the people who had voted against my proposal came to me after the meeting, with tears in her eyes, to apologize for disagreeing with me. I assured her that I still loved her, that we were still friends, and that we both were still Christians. Neither of us was wrong; we had just seen things differently.

Our churches do not deal very well with conflict. Perhaps in large measure this is because we insist on seeing the world in terms of either/or, of winning or losing. But that is not the only way, or even the best way, to view our conflicts. Sometimes the truth is both/and, without the need for winners or losers.

We would be mistaken if we concluded that because James and Paul have different emphases, one of them must be right and the other must be wrong. In truth, James and Paul are both right. Sometimes we need to hear Paul's reassurance of God's love and grace despite our sin. Sometimes we need James to call us to task for our spiritual laziness and laxity. We always need to remember that faith and works are two complementary expressions of one life in Christ.

LESSON PLAN

■ After your opening prayer, write on a chalkboard or on a large piece of paper "Can faith save you?" Ask for responses. Most class members will probably say, Yes; of course salvation comes through faith. Some may quote Scripture: "Your faith has saved you" (Luke 7:50) or, "For by grace you have been saved through faith" (Ephesians 2:8). Now read the question in its context, in James 2:14. Ask for responses. Some members may still insist that salvation, after all, comes through faith, not through works. Others may observe that faith that does not show itself in good works is not really faith. Summarize for your class the claim made above, that James does not contrast faith with works but rather contrasts true faith with false faith.

Invite a class member to read aloud James 2:15-17. Then ask: ***Does this situation sound familiar? If so, why?*** (*Undoubtedly, it will; who hasn't passed a beggar on the street or a homeless person sleeping in the open with no place to go? Likely, however, someone will observe that often such people are responsible for their own fate and that we have no way of knowing that they would not use any money we gave them to buy alcohol or other drugs.*) Notice that James does not say that we should give money to every needy person we see. What he says is that mere sympathy and best wishes are no help at all. The challenge is to get involved. James's point is that faith that does not make a difference is not true faith: "Faith by itself, if it has no works, is dead" (2:17).

Now ask someone to read aloud James 2:18. James clearly believes that true faith will show itself by works. Have the class consider silently the question at the end of the introduction to the section in the student book entitled "Faithful Living" [page 26]: "What do your works tell others about your faith?" After about a minute, ask: ***How does this question make you feel?*** (*Many class members will likely say that they feel uneasy or guilty. Others may say that they feel challenged to live their life in accordance with their faith.*)

Returning to the question on the chalkboard or large piece of paper, circle the word "faith." Ask: ***What do you think the word* faith *means?*** (*Some may say that it means belief. Notice, though, James's point that mere belief, which does not show itself in a transformed life, can scarcely be called "faith." James, indeed, describes the "faith" [better, "belief"] of the demons. They know who God is, but that knowledge does not transform them. Saving faith must be something more than mere belief. Someone will likely cite the definition of faith in Hebrews 11:1: "Now faith is the assurance of things hoped for, the conviction of things not seen." Note that this famous definition, too, goes beyond mere belief to conviction and commitment. Finally, if no one else does, observe that faith includes an element of risk. We do not need to have faith in the things we can see and touch. Faith calls us to trust in what we cannot see and to act upon our trust.*)

James illustrates this point with two biblical examples: Abraham and Rahab. Before the session familiarize yourself with the stories to which James refers from Genesis 22:1-19 and Joshua 2:1-21; 6:22-25. Be prepared to retell these stories if the class is unfamiliar with them. Note also the story of Jean Buchanan on page 27 in the student book as a contemporary example of a person who, like Abraham and Rahab, lived her faith. Ask the question on that page: ***"What 'friend of God' has been an important influence or a blessing in your life?"*** (*Many answers are possible: parents, spouses, pastors, old saints of the church.*) Now ask: ***What do these people's lives have in common?*** (*Note that in every case these are people whose Christianity was apparent to everyone by the way they lived their lives—or, in James's terms, people who showed their faith by their works.*)

Drawing on the discussions in the student book [pages 28–29] and above, summarize for your class the controversy between James and Paul concerning faith and works. You will want to look up the texts from Paul's letters mentioned in the two discussions. Indeed, you may want to have your class consult some of these texts and then ask the members how they think James and Paul compare.

To organize this summary, make two columns on

a chalkboard or large piece of paper headed "Faith" and "Works"; then make two rows within each of the columns labeled "James" and "Paul." Consider first of all what James and Paul mean when they use the term *faith* (For James, you could write "belief"; for Paul, you could write "commitment."). Next, fill in the ways that these two Christian thinkers use the word *works* (Write "deeds of love" for James, "works of the law" for Paul.). Or you could prepare this chart before the session as a poster and use it to illustrate your summary. Note that although James and Paul have different emphases, they are not contradictory. Both would agree that saving faith produces a life of good works.

Now turn to the final section of the Bible passage, on faith in action in the community. Point out that James urges believers to share their suffering and their joy with the community of faith. Ask: ***Do we share our sorrows and joys with one another?*** (*Some class members may say that they do feel able to share. Others, however, may be less certain.*) Then ask: ***What fears keep us from sharing freely with one another?*** (*Some members may say that fear of rejection or fear of broken confidences keeps them from sharing. Others may say that they are afraid to share because they do not believe that anyone will understand.*) Retell the story on page 29 in the student book of the six women in the same Sunday school class who all had suffered abuse but who had never shared their pain. Observe that, for James, the church is meant to be a community of love and acceptance that ministers to us in our pain as well as in our joy.

Finally, ask someone to read aloud James 5:16. Then ask: ***What does it mean that the prayer of a righteous person "is powerful and effective"?*** (*Some may say that this means God answers the prayers of good people. However, all of us know good people whose prayers have not been answered. Others will discern that power in prayer is not a magical ability to get whatever we ask for. Rather, power in prayer means an openness and sensitivity to God so that whatever comes, we know that God is with us.*)

Close the session by having the class sing the hymn "Dear Jesus, in Whose Life I See."

[1] From "Reading the Mail," by Martin E. Marty, in *The Christian Century*, Vol. 112, No. 19, June 7-14, 1995; page 623.

TRY ANOTHER METHOD

■ The concluding verses of our Bible passage deal with prayer for healing. You may want to ask people in your class to share their own experiences of healing. Perhaps you could invite someone to come to the session and to witness to God's healing power in his or her life. Or you and your class may want to visit a healing service in an area church. If you do this, however, be sure to allow time for debriefing so that you can talk about the experience and how it fits with your own experience of who God is and how God acts.

Whichever of these options you pursue, make sure you and your class members always keep in mind that prayer for healing is prayer, not magic. God is not some neutral power, subject to our control. God is the Lord of heaven and earth before whom every knee must bow. The language of prayer is the language of petition, not of command.

Chapter Four

LETTING WISDOM GUIDE

PURPOSE

To help us act with the gentle, peaceable, and caring wisdom that comes from above

BIBLE PASSAGE

James 1:5-8; 3:1-5a, 13-18

CORE VERSE

Who is wise and understanding among you? Show by your good life that your works are done with gentleness born of wisdom. (James 3:13)

GET READY

■ You may be disturbed to read James's advice on teaching: "Not many of you should become teachers, my brothers and sisters" (3:1). As a teacher himself, James had a high view of his calling and of the responsibilities it entails. What James certainly also knew, but does not relate to us, are the great rewards of teaching: among them, the joy of watching your students open their minds to new ways of seeing and different ways of understanding.

As you prepare for the session, be sure to take time to thank God for calling you to teach. Pray for greater sensitivity to the responsibilities you have as a teacher. In particular, pray that God will grant you wisdom so that you will not only teach facts about the faith but will also guide your class members into a deeper life of faith.

BIBLE BACKGROUND

■ **James 1:5.** "Wisdom" is a difficult concept to define. Both the Hebrew *chokmah* and the Greek *sophia* are words with good and bad connotations. *Sophia*, for example, can refer to the wisdom of this world rather than the wisdom of God (1 Corinthians 1:20); and the Hebrew term can be used for someone crafty and devious (2 Samuel 13:3). However, in the Wisdom Literature of ancient Israel, wisdom took on a particular meaning. In Proverbs the wise are those who know how to live rightly and well. The wise have insight into the pattern at the heart of reality. Understanding the meaning of life, they are able to structure their lives accordingly. And in the words of the sages of Israel, such wisdom can come only from God:

> For the LORD gives wisdom;
> from his mouth come knowledge
> and understanding.
> (Proverbs 2:6)

When James says that the one who lacks wisdom should ask God, he stands solidly in the Wisdom tradition of Israel.

Wisdom and knowledge are by no means synonymous. Knowledge can contribute to wisdom, but wisdom requires something more than the amassing of facts. For example, I know that being overweight is bad for me. I also know that, genetics and body chemistry notwithstanding, the major reason I am overweight is that I eat too much and exercise too little. That is knowledge. For me actually to do something about it—to eat less and to begin an exercise regimen—would be wisdom. Knowledge comes fairly easily. Wisdom is hard.

Sadly, human history is filled with tragic illustrations of the failure of knowledgeable people to act wisely. As the Israeli diplomat Abba Eban has observed, "History teaches us that men and nations behave wisely once they have exhausted all other alternatives."[1] The student book mentions failed social programs such as government housing projects and ecological disasters such as the widespread use of DDT. The lesson has been taught us again and again, but still we fail to learn wisdom—perhaps because we have forgotten where wisdom comes from. As James and the sages of Israel taught, wisdom comes only from God. The first step in attaining wisdom, then, is recognizing that we need to ask God for it.

As the student book observes, James's confidence that we may ask God for wisdom also reflects the teaching of Jesus in the Sermon on the Mount. In Matthew 7:7-11, Jesus urges his followers to ask confidently; for "if you . . . know how to give good gifts to your children, how much more will your Father in heaven give good things to those who ask him!" (Matthew 7:11). Knowing that God "gives to all generously and ungrudgingly" (James 1:5), we can approach God confidently in prayer.

Verses 6-8. What does it mean to "ask in faith, never doubting"? At first, one might conclude that it means really believing you will get what you ask for—thinking positively, in other words. However, remember that in the Book of James faith is never just a matter of believing. Faith involves the commitment of one's whole life. Therefore, to pray "in faith" means to address God with wholehearted devotion. The point is not that if you believe, you will get what you pray for. Rather, the point is that the one who seeks wisdom must do so from a standpoint of faith.

When James speaks of doubting, he does not mean doubting that the prayer will be answered. He means doubting God, doubting that God "gives to all generously and ungrudgingly" (1:5). James compares such a doubter to "a wave of the sea, driven and tossed by the wind" (1:6): inconstant, faithless, without stability or direction. This analogy would have been particularly significant in the ancient world. For many ancient Near Eastern peoples, the sea was the symbol of chaos and disorder, opposed to the ordering, creative work of the gods. Refusal to trust God, then, means abandoning the very pattern and meaning of the world. It means letting go of order and surrendering to chaos.

If we do not believe that God can be trusted, we will hedge our bets by trying to follow the world's wisdom as well as God's. That is why James calls such people "double-minded" (James Hardy Ropes suggests reading it "Mr. Facing-both-ways"![2]). We have already seen that James has no patience for casual Christianity. Double-minded people, who try to hold on to heaven and earth at the same time, will wind up with neither. James says that they "must not expect to receive anything from the Lord" (1:7-8).

James 3:1-5a. Once more we move from a general principle to its application in the life of the church. Teachers are particularly responsible for preserving and communicating the wisdom of God. Therefore, they will be judged more strictly than anyone else. Moreover, teachers must hold themselves to a high standard. They must be particularly careful because the teacher's instrument, the tongue, is the most devious and dangerous organ of the body (James 3:5b-12). When James speaks of "mak[ing] mistakes" (3:2), he is not referring particularly to errors of fact. He is speaking, rather, of failure to control our speech, of speaking harmfully or irresponsibly. James regards control of the spoken word as essential. The person who can control his or her tongue, James asserts, "is perfect, able to keep the whole body in check with a bridle" (3:2).

The Greek word translated "perfect" here is *teleios*, a favorite word of James (1:4, 17, 25). *Teleios* is also found in Matthew 5:48: "Be perfect, therefore, as your heavenly father is perfect." Here as there, *teleios* does not mean perfect in the sense that we often mean, that is, entirely without mistakes or errors. Rather, it means "whole, complete, entire." The word is translated "mature" in James 1:4. Controlling the tongue is an essential step in Christian wholeness and maturity.

To illustrate his point that controlling the tongue results in the control of the whole person, James uses the example of a horse, which can be steered by its rider through a bridle and bit placed in the horse's mouth (3:2-3). Similarly, pilots are able to steer great ships by means of "a very small rudder" (3:4). The imagery of sailing ships and horses belongs to the Greek-speaking world of James's day. However, the power of the tongue to do either great good or incalculable harm was well-known by the sages of ancient Israel. The illustrations from Proverbs cited in the student book [pages 35–36] barely scratch the surface.

Is this making too much of the potential of words for good and for harm? Consider the example of Adolf Hitler, cited in the student book. Through his hate-filled rhetoric, Hitler was able to inflame his people with such zeal that they nearly conquered all Europe—

and was able so to deaden their consciences that they slaughtered millions of innocent people. Lest we think that Hitler's Germany was some kind of historical mistake, an aberration that could never happen again, consider the terrorists who blew up the Federal Building in Oklahoma City in the spring of 1995. Those wicked, misguided zealots were acting out the hateful ranting of extremists here at home—people who say that they cannot be held responsible for mere words. James reminds us, however, that "mere" words carry tremendous power.

If we are still unconvinced of this truth, we need only consider Jesus of Nazareth. Jesus did not invent anything or build anything material that has lasted to our time. He founded no political movement, wrote no books or poems, created no lasting works of art. Mainly, what he did was talk; and his words are still ringing down the centuries, carrying the transforming power of his message and his person to us today and onward into the future. When James said that the tongue "boasts of great exploits" (3:5), he made one of the great understatements of all time. Far more accurate is the opening phrase of John's Gospel: "In the beginning was the Word."

Verses 13-18. In the last lesson we saw that, for James, true faith is revealed by a life of good works. The same is true of wisdom; as with faith, the acid test is the way life is lived. Once more, James issues his challenge: "Show by your good life that your works are done with gentleness born of wisdom" (3:13). As the student book rightly observes, "Gentleness is not a quality greatly admired and sought after in today's world" [page 37]. In James's day as well, the qualities of cutthroat competition—of envy and ambition—were far more prized. James, however, does not hesitate to attribute such worldly wisdom to its proper source: "Such wisdom does not come down from above, but is earthly, unspiritual, devilish" (3:15).

Of course, one could claim that a life of gentleness and peace, as attractive as it sounds, is impractical. People who are involved in the real world simply cannot afford the luxury of living that way. To get ahead, to succeed, we have to use the world's tactics. James, on the contrary, insists that it is the devilish "wisdom" of ambition and envy that is impractical: "For where there is envy and selfish ambition, there will also be disorder and wickedness of every kind" (3:16). The self-centered, "practical" wisdom of the world produces pain, inequality, and anger. Only when we act "impractically," by thinking of the needs of others and acting for the common good, do we find true success.

In the area where I live, there is a chain of family-owned grocery stores. The owners are committed Christians who are active in local charities. The stores do not sell alcoholic beverages. They are closed on Sundays and on all major holidays so employees can spend time with their families. Yet these stores are among the most successful in the area. Perhaps, after all, cutthroat competition is not the only way to success.

James concludes with a description of the wisdom that is from above (3:17-18). The characteristics of that true wisdom sound a great deal like those Paul ascribes to love in 1 Corinthians 13. This should not be surprising. After all, if God is love, then the divine wisdom will surely be revealed in a life of love. James 3 ends up with a glowing promise for the person who, acting in the loving, gentle wisdom of God, makes peace in the world. For such a one, "a harvest of righteousness is sown in peace" (3:18). No wonder Jesus said, "Blessed are the peacemakers, for they will be called children of God" (Matthew 5:9).

INTRODUCE OUR NEED

■ When we drive from our home in Virginia to visit my wife's parents in New Jersey, we pass through the state of Maryland. The highway patrols of many states have posted signs urging folks to drive safely and within the speed limits. But Maryland's signs are special—as those of you who have driven in Maryland know. There, the signs read, "Please Drive Gently."

James would approve. Gentleness, he reminds us, is a hallmark of "the wisdom from above" (3:17). Unfortunately, we do not have many role models for gentle driving—or for gentle living.

As the student book reminds us, our popular culture does not prize gentleness, probably because we equate gentleness with weakness. However, nothing could be further from the truth. True strength shows itself, not in violence, but in gentleness. There was no weakness in Martin Luther King, Jr.'s refusal to match violence with violence as he led march after march for civil rights. There was nothing weak about Mother Teresa, moving fearlessly through the alleys and gutters of Calcutta to minister to the poorest of the world's poor. Nor was there any weakness in the One who laid down his life for the sins of the whole world on Calvary. As the apostle Paul said, though the cross seems weak and foolish to the world, "God's foolishness is wiser than human wisdom, and God's weakness is stronger than human strength" (1 Corinthians 1:25). May God guide us into that wisdom that expresses itself in a life of gentleness and peace and mutual care.

LESSON PLAN

■ Following your opening prayer, write the word "wise" on a chalkboard or on a large piece of paper. Ask: ***What comes to mind when you see this word?*** (*Clearly, many answers are possible. Class members may call out "smart," "intelligent," "the three wise men," "Solomon," or others. If no negative illustrations are brought forward, prompt the class by suggesting some: "wise guy," "wise crack," "wiseacre."*) Point out that the Greek and Hebrew words for "wisdom" are also ambiguous terms. However, as James uses the word, *wisdom* appears to mean what it meant to the sages of ancient Israel who gave us the Book of Proverbs. In both cases wisdom means insight into the meaning of the world and the ability to live in accordance with the meaning of things—in short, we might call wisdom "the ability to live rightly and well."

Ask: ***Does wisdom mean the same thing as knowledge?*** (*Some members may say that these words do have the same meaning. Others, though, will note that knowing the right thing to do and doing it are two very different things. The student book gives several examples of actions that seemed wise at the time, based on our knowledge, but turned out disastrously. Your class will likely have other illustrations.*)

Point out that, according to James and to Israel's sages, wisdom is a gift given by God. Then ask the question at the end of the introduction to the section in the student book entitled "Faithful Living" [page 34]: ***"In what areas of your life do you need wisdom from God?"*** (*Some class members may answer that they need wisdom in Bible study or in knowing God's will for their lives. Others may be more specific and personal, telling of needing God's guidance in job hunting, in finding a life partner, in dealing with their family, or in their workplace. If responses are slow in coming or are overly vague, tell a relevant story from your own life.*)

Ask a class member to read aloud James 1:6-8. Then ask: ***Does James say that if we ask in faith and do not doubt, we will get whatever we pray for?*** (*Some, indeed many, class members are likely to say yes.*) Now ask: ***Is this true to our experience?*** (*Some may still insist that whenever they asked in faith, they received what they asked for. Most, however, will acknowledge that all too often prayers of faith—especially prayers for healing—have not been answered.*)

Remind your class of the discussion in the last session on faith and works. Remember that, for James, faith must be more than mere belief. It makes sense, then, that praying "in faith" means something more than having an unswerving belief that we will get what we want. Summarize the discussion above on faith and doubt in prayer. Then write the word "double-minded" on a chalkboard or large piece of paper. Ask: ***What do you think it means to be "double-minded"?*** (*Some possible responses are "trying to have it both ways," "sitting on the fence," "two-faced," "indecisive," or "insincere."*) James says that the "double-minded" person cannot expect anything from God. In particular, wisdom must be sought from a position of wholehearted devotion to God and a wholehearted desire to know God's will.

Move on now to wisdom in speaking. Ask someone to read aloud James 3:1. Then ask: ***Why does James say that teachers "will be judged with greater strictness"?*** (*The reason given in the text is linked to common human failure: "For all of us make many mistakes" [James 3:2].*) But why should the mistakes of teachers be more serious than mistakes made by others? Read or retell the story of "Squeak School" from the student book. Notice especially the mother's caution to her son that "a teacher's first responsibility is to avoid leading his or her students astray" [page 35]. When a teacher errs, the error is compounded by being passed on to others, who may in turn mislead others. So it is particularly important for teachers to be closely tied to the source of truth and wisdom.

Ask someone to read aloud James 3:3-5a. Then consider the excerpts from Proverbs found on page 36 in the student book. Notice the similarities between James and Proverbs concerning the power of the tongue to change lives for good or ill. Ask the first question at the end of the section in the student book entitled "Speak Wisely" [page 37]: ***"What words have blessed you?"*** (*Class members are likely to recall encouragement that they received from parents, friends, family members, teachers, youth leaders, pastors, or others. Some may share recent examples of how they have been encouraged by positive words.*)

Follow up with the second question: ***"How are your words a blessing to others?"*** (*Likely, this will be a sobering question. We are all aware of how easy it is to lash out unthinkingly with hurtful words when we are angry or upset. Consider, too, the effect that thoughtless gossip has on the lives and reputations of innocent people. Read James 3:2 aloud, explaining that "perfect" here means spiritually complete and mature. James assures us that control of the tongue makes us whole. For our spiritual growth, we must learn to speak words of blessing, not curse.*)

Write the word "gentleness" on a chalkboard or large piece of paper, and ask the class members what this word brings to their minds. Write the responses on the chalkboard or large piece of paper. Chances are, most responses will be on the order of "kind," "loving," "soft," "meek." It is likely that no one will suggest "strong" or "successful" as words that "gentleness" brings to mind. Point this out to the class; then ask: ***Is gentleness unrealistic in today's world?*** (*While no one is likely to agree absolutely, most class members will probably say that it is hard to be gentle in a world as harsh and competitive as ours.*)

Ask a class member to read aloud James 3:15-16. James argues that what is impractical is the self-centeredness born of "envy and selfish ambition" that the world calls "wisdom." James asserts that such wisdom is devilish in origin and produces "disorder and wickedness of every kind" (3:16). Consider the examples of corporate disarray and neighborhood violence given in the student book. Clearly, the practical way of self-interest is neither practical nor in our own best interests. Only the wisdom "from above," based on love and respect for the neighbor, can yield a society of blessing and peace.

Ask the question at the end of the lesson in the student book: ***"How can you make a difference by acting with wisdom that is gentle and peaceable?"*** (*People will offer various suggestions, and there may be disagreement. Nonetheless, urge your class to think of concrete ways that we can teach, not violence, but gentleness and peace. One real possibility may be volunteering as a class to work with youth in your church or neighborhood. Talk to your church youth director about ways your group may be able to help.*)

James affirms that if we ask in faith for wisdom, God will respond "generously and ungrudgingly" (1:5). To celebrate the certainty of God's guidance and wisdom, have the class sing "This Is a Day of New Beginnings." Then pray together the prayer at the end of the student book lesson.

[1] Speech in London, December 16, 1970. From *The Oxford Dictionary of Modern Quotations*, edited by Tony Augarde (Oxford University Press, 1991); page 71.

[2] From *A Critical and Exegetical Commentary on the Book of James*, by James Hardy Ropes in the International Critical Commentary Series (T. & T. Clark, 1997); page 143.

TRY ANOTHER METHOD

■ James, who took seriously the hardships and responsibilities of teaching, cautions us that "not many . . . should become teachers" (3:1). You may want to consider inviting a Christian teacher in the public schools or in an area college to your class to share with you the reason he or she feels called to teach and some of the joys and challenges of that special profession. This could also be a good Sunday to ask your Sunday school superintendent or director of Christian education to speak briefly about the educational ministry in your church. Your class may want to volunteer time to help out in the Sunday school or in a summer vacation Bible school program as a way of supporting this vital ministry.

This would be a good week to think about recognizing people in your church who have embodied the peaceable wisdom James describes. In last week's lesson, Ms. Pat Floyd, writer of our student book, described how her church had celebrated "Jean Buchanan Day," honoring a woman whose life had been an example to many. Surely, in your church there is such a person. Consider having a church supper or other celebration to honor that someone in your church whose life demonstrates the qualities of wisdom James describes.

James urges us to control our speech and to listen. A good way to put this into practice would be to try some exercises in silence. Close the session with a period of silent prayer—not the thirty seconds or so that we usually allow for silence in worship, but a full two-to-five minutes of silence. Or encourage your class members to devote two-to-five minutes a day this week to silent meditation. See what begins to happen as you deliberately take time to listen for God's presence in your life.

Talk with your pastor and the chairperson of your worship committee about planning a worship service structured around silence. Arrange for Scripture readings and meditative hymns interspersed with long periods of silence for prayer and meditation.

Chapter Five

DOING RIGHT

PURPOSE

To deepen our capacity and strengthen our resolve to do right

BIBLE PASSAGE

James 4:1-10, 13-17

> **CORE VERSE**
> Anyone, then, who knows the right thing to do and fails to do it, commits sin. (James 4:17)

GET READY

■ In the previous lesson, we heard some stern warnings about the false, self-centered wisdom of this world. In this lesson as our study of the Book of James comes to an end, the writer continues on that same theme, linking the conflicts and disputes that tear us apart to the selfish desires within us. As always, for James the way out is clear. We should simply do what we already know to be right: submit to God and live a life given to others, not to self.

However, the right thing to do may not be quite so clear for your class members—or for you. The good news is that, as James assures us, God is always ready to offer guidance and direction to those who ask in faith. As you prepare, pray for the class members—especially for those who are searching for God's guidance this week in particular difficulties. Ask God to give you the wisdom to be teacher and friend to them in their searching.

BIBLE BACKGROUND

■ **James 4:1-3.** This lesson continues the theme of dealing with conflict, which was introduced in James 3:13-18. In those verses James affirms that the wise person will be found engaged in making peace rather than in causing conflict. This is because the wisdom of God is peaceful and gentle, in sharp contrast to the "bitter envy and selfish ambition" (3:14) that characterize worldly wisdom. In James 4:1-3, conflicts and disputes in our lives are traced to that same envy and ambition.

As the student book suggests, commentators have long puzzled over the word *murder* in James 4:2. It does seem a bit extreme to go directly from envy to killing. Some, as a result, have suggested that the word *murder* has been put here by mistake or that James is exaggerating to make his point more dramatically. However, the student book reminds us that murder can indeed be the end result of envy. Remember, too, Jesus' teaching on murder: "You have heard that it was said to those of ancient times, 'You shall not murder'; and 'whoever murders shall be liable to judgment.' But I say to you that if you are angry with a brother or sister, you will be liable to judgment; and if you insult a brother or sister, you will be liable to the council; and if you say, 'You fool,' you will be liable to the hell of fire" (Matthew 5:21-22).

For James as for Jesus, murder is the end result of failing to live by the gentle and peaceable wisdom of God. To hate others is already to murder them in our hearts.

You may recall that coveting, which James identifies as the beginning of our "disputes and conflicts" (4:2), is forbidden by the Ten Commandments (Exodus

20:17; Deuteronomy 5:21). To covet something is to want it so badly that you begin to think of ways to make that thing yours—in other words, to want it so badly that you disregard the feelings and rights of its owner. Coveting is thus the first stage of theft and leads to envy. Envy (discussed in James 3:13-18) is closely connected to coveting. However, envy is directed, not at the possession, but at the person: "I covet what you have; I envy you for having it." We often use this word playfully: "I envy you; you have such lovely children." However, there is nothing playful about the real thing. Envy does not mean admiring another's good fortune or even wishing that good fortune could be yours. Envy means despising the other for having what you do not. In envy, resentment builds to hatred or even (as the student book grimly reminds us) to murder. By warning us sternly against coveting, James intends to keep us from starting on this dangerous road.

The heart of coveting and envy is wanting what we do not have. James asserts, however, that "you do not have, because you do not ask" (4:2). Asking, after all, requires humility. It means acknowledging our need and submitting to the other by recognizing his or her right to give or not. Most especially, asking means recognizing our debt to the giver. No wonder the wisdom of this world prefers taking to asking.

Of course, one might object to James's assertion. It is simply not the case that the only reason for not having is not asking. Many who ask still do not receive. The issue we are facing here, then, is related to the discussion of asking in faith in James 1:5-8. There James notes that the one who asks (from the context, for wisdom specifically) will not receive unless asking "in faith, never doubting" (1:6). In Lesson 4, we observed that this is much more than a call to positive thinking. To ask in faith is to ask out of a life lived in obedience to God. Only in that context can the prayer for wisdom be answered, for only the one who is obedient to God truly desires to be wise.

So also here, in James 4:3, we are told, "You ask and do not receive, because you ask wrongly, in order to spend what you get on your pleasures." James reminds us that *what we want depends upon who we are.* If we are slaves to the craving within us, living lives of envy and strife, then our desire will be selfish. Our prayers will be, not genuine attempts to seek God's will, but wish lists thrown at the heavens. On the other hand, if we pray "in faith," we will want what God wants and what we ask will be in harmony with God's will. The Book of James is not a primer on how to get what we want out of God. It is a guide to becoming the people God calls us to be.

Verses 4-6. These verses begin by addressing the readers as "Adulterers"—actually "Adulteresses," since the Greek word is feminine. As the student book observes, this does not mean that James is accusing his readers of sexual immorality. Rather, adultery is here used to symbolize unfaithfulness to God, as the remainder of verse 4 reveals: "Do you not know that friendship with the world is enmity with God? Therefore whoever wishes to be a friend of the world becomes an enemy of God."

In the ancient world, cities and nations were symbolically described as women, being the mothers of their inhabitants, and were often understood to be "wed" to a god. Similarly, the people of Israel were seen by the prophets as the bride of the Lord (Jeremiah 2:2; Hosea 2:19-20). Therefore, when Israel turned to other gods or trusted in foreign alliances rather than in God, this act was deemed adultery; and Israel was condemned as an adulteress (Jeremiah 9:2-3; Hosea 3:1; and the graphic, deliberately offensive depiction of Jerusalem's adultery in Ezekiel 16). In the New Testament it is the church that has become the bride of Christ (Ephesians 5:22-33; Revelation 19:9; 21:2). So when James calls his readers "adulteresses," he is standing in the ancient prophetic tradition of Israel.

James continues in this vein in verse 5, where God's call to exclusive devotion is demonstrated by a quote: "God yearns jealously for the spirit that he has made to dwell in us." This is a difficult verse, and the quote does not appear to come from any Scripture text known to us. The idea that God has made a spirit "to dwell in us" is not found in the Hebrew Bible. However, it is found in some early Christian writings, for instance, "The Shepherd of Hermas," a text often compared to James (See the article "James: The Man and the Book," pages 5–7 in this publication.).

The idea of divine jealousy is a familiar biblical theme. In Exodus 20:5, the Lord's demand for exclusive worship is explained: "For I the LORD your God am a jealous God." The Hebrew word translated "jealous" here, *qanna'*, has to do with strong emotion or passion, as does the Greek word *phthonos* used in James 4:5. We might perhaps better say that the Lord is a **zealous** God, passionately committed to God's people—"to the thousandth generation of those who love me and keep my commandments" (Exodus 20:6). Knowing the divine zeal, James says, we should also know that God takes our commitment seriously.

The quotation in James 4:6 *is* from the Bible—from Proverbs 3:34, to be exact. However, the form in which it appears here will not closely resemble that passage from our Old Testament. That is because James is citing the text, not from the Hebrew Bible, but as it appears in the Septuagint, a Greek translation of the Jewish Scriptures done in Egypt around the second century B.C. In any case, the meaning of the text is clear. If we in selfish pride insist upon our own way, God is against us. But, if in humility we recognize our need, the God who "gives grace to the humble" (James 4:6) will be for us.

Verses 7-10. Here we find James's remedy for the conflicts that tear at us. First, "Submit yourselves therefore to God" (4:7). It is interesting to note that the Arabic word *Islam* means "submission" and that a Muslim is, in Arabic, "one who submits" to the will of God. Perhaps we Christian believers need to learn that we too are called to submit—to the lordship of Jesus Christ. Remember that James identifies himself in James 1:1 as "a servant [literally, "slave"] of God and of the Lord Jesus Christ." If we are to find the grace of God powerfully at work in us, we too must become slaves of God, submitting our wills to God's will as revealed in Jesus Christ.

Second, James says, "Resist the devil" (4:7). We must declare our allegiance to God and reject the enemy or remain friends of the world and reject God. We cannot be "double-minded," with one foot in each camp (James 1:8; 4:8). The good news is that we actually can resist evil. Many believers through the centuries have painted lurid pictures of the demonic powers, presenting Satan as only a little less powerful than God. James does not deny the dangerous and seductive power of the enemy. He affirms, however, that believers can be victorious: "Resist the devil, and he will flee from you" (4:7).

Third, James admonishes us, "Draw near to God, and he will draw near to you" (4:8). Our faith is not simply a matter of deciding, once and for all, to submit to God and resist the devil. The decision is forced upon us again and again, moment by moment. Yet, in the living of our faith, James assures us that we need never be alone. If we desire to draw near to God, we can be certain that God is drawing near to us to strengthen us and bring us through.

In a word, what James describes here is repentance: turning away from life as we have lived it and turning toward the new life to which God calls us and for which God empowers us. This can be no casual decision. James says, "Lament and mourn and weep. Let your laughter be turned into mourning and your joy into dejection" (4:9). If our repentance is to be genuine, our sorrow over our past sins must be no less genuine. However, James promises, "Humble yourselves before the Lord, and he will exalt you" (4:10).

Verses 13-17. In these verses we are shown a good example of the kind of halfhearted faith James deplores. It is important to realize that James does not object to planning ahead, to traveling, or to making money. What angers him in this illustration is the complete failure of the person described either to ask for or to desire God's guidance. Rather, the person in the illustration simply assumes that God must approve of these plans. This, James says, is arrogant boasting; and "all such boasting is evil" (4:16). Instead, we must learn to seek God's guidance and God's will each day in all that we do.

The final words in James 4 serve as a fitting conclusion to our study of James: "Anyone, then, who knows the right thing to do and fails to do it, commits sin" (4:17). Usually, when we think of sin, we think of committing specific immoral acts. Being righteous, by this way of thinking, is primarily a negative: If you don't smoke, drink, swear, or fool around, then you are a good person. This definition of righteousness and sin also lends itself to self-righteousness, as people who have not yet succumbed to these particular public temptations look smugly at those who have.

James, however, says that it is not righteousness but sin that is defined by negatives. If we do not do those deeds of love and kindness we know we should do, that is sin. By this definition, righteousness is defined by what you do, not by what you avoid. Nor is there any room to be found here for self-righteousness, for there are always more deeds of love to be done; we can never be said to be finished. James, in short, gives a program for our entire lifetime. For James, faith is life.

INTRODUCE OUR NEED

■ In the first year or so after Wendy and I were married, I dealt with conflict by denying it. Instead of arguing, I would leave the room. Instead of fighting, I would sit in silence. I was pleased with myself for acting so maturely and avoiding conflict.

But, of course, I was not avoiding conflict at all. I was fighting, all right—fighting dirty, with distance and silence as my weapons. Anger and resentment built up inside me, and the cold silences grew and grew. Then one day I realized what I was doing. I was pouting! There was nothing good or noble in my behavior and certainly nothing mature. Of course, once I had put the right name to my behavior, I could not do it anymore. Wendy and I began to talk out our differences and to deal more healthily with our conflicts.

James is a blunt little book. It forces us to face up to what we are really doing and to what our motives really are. Are we involved in conflicts and disputes today in our families or churches or communities? James says that, whatever fancy names we may use to dignify our disagreements, most of them boil down to the same thing: "your cravings that are at war within you" (4:1). Put simply, we want our own way. Like children fighting over a shiny toy, we refuse to share. Our petty disputes can erupt into deadly violence or frost over into hatred and isolation. The end result is brokenness: broken families, broken dreams, broken lives.

Blunt as James is about the problem, he is also clear on the remedy: "Submit yourselves therefore to God. . . . Draw near to God, and he will draw near to you" (4:7-8). As long as we continue to be self-centered, we will resent the successes of others and want what they have. The only way we can find peace is by giving our lives to God and living for others. Only then can we discover the joy God created us to know.

LESSON PLAN

■ After your opening prayer, relate the story from the student book about the thirteen-year-old boy who was killed for his shoes and jacket [page 42]. Or you may want to relate a similar incident, closer to home, from your own area newspapers. Ask: ***Why do tragedies like this happen?*** (*Some of the class members may give answers relating to religious concepts, such as human sin and rebellion. Others may give social reasons: poverty, poor education, or the prevalence of violence in the media. And still others may point out the social dimensions of human sin.*) When several have shared, read aloud James 4:1-2b (ending with "conflicts"). Ask: ***How does James explain the existence of conflicts and disputes among us?*** (*The answer, of course, is "your cravings that are at war within you" [James 4:1].*) Reflect on what James means by this, reminding the class of the last lesson's discussion of the peaceable wisdom of God contrasted with the "bitter envy and selfish ambition" (James 3:14) of this world's wisdom.

Note the controversy over the word *murder* in James 4:2. Ask: ***Do you believe James is exaggerating here? Why or why not?*** (*Some class members may well think that James is, but others will cite your opening illustration as demonstration that envy can ultimately lead to murder.*) Read aloud the text from Matthew 5:21-22 cited above to show that Jesus also made this connection between violence and inner turmoil.

Ask someone to read aloud James 4:2c-3 (beginning with "You do not have"). Note the similarity between this text and James 1:5-8. Observe that in each case James is not telling us how to manipulate God into giving us what we want. James's concern, rather, is that we conform to God's will.

Summarize the discussion above and in the student book [pages 43-44] on unfaithfulness as "adultery," referring to the illustrations from the Hebrew Bible (particularly those from Hosea). Then ask someone to read aloud James 4:4. Ask: ***When do the priorities we choose for ourselves make us "a friend of the world," to use James's term? How do we know when "friendship with the world" becomes "enmity with God"?*** (*Class members may respond with blatant examples, such as lying and cheating in business, or with more subtle ones, such as never mentioning Jesus to your coworkers or living extravagantly when others are in need.*) Cite the illustration of the writer's new home in the section in the student book entitled "God or the World?" and ask if this represents compromising with the world. (*Some class members may insist that it does, that the money should have been given to the poor. However, others will probably say that having a beautiful place to live need not mean that one is being unfaithful to God. To the contrary, the promise in James 4:10 is that those who are humble before God will be exalted.*)

Turn to the description of repentance in James 4:7-10. Move through the three-part summary in James 4:7-8 of what repentance entails ([1] Submit to God. [2] Resist the devil. [3] Draw near to God.), writing the points on a chalkboard or large piece of paper as you discuss them. Note in particular James's insistence that we must choose either to follow God and resist the devil or to follow the devil and resist God.

Point out the term *double-minded* in James 4:8. Ask your class to recall the discussion of this term from the last session, guiding them where they are uncertain. Here as in James 1:8, James rejects the double-minded, calling upon them to purify their hearts. Note that "purifying" means eliminating waste until only one thing is left. Pure gold is gold from which all the impurities have been purged, leaving only gold. Just so, a pure heart is a heart devoted only to God.

Next, invite class members to consider their own resistance to sin. Ask: ***What has been your experience in resisting sin?*** (*Some class members may speak generally of struggling with temptation or of praying for strength. Others may describe specific victories in their life—when God delivered them from addiction or helped them forgive an enemy.*) Ask a class member to read or retell the illustration from *The Tribe of the Tiger* in the student book [pages 45-46]. Emphasize James's assurance of victory over the enemy: "Resist the devil, and he will flee from you" (James 4:7).

Finally, observe that drawing near to God is a day-to-day experience. For that reason the attitude of the person in James 4:13 is not the attitude of faith. As the student book observes, "When we make plans for what we will do each day, we need to ask, "What would God have me do?' " [page 47]. Ask someone to read aloud James 4:17. Summarize the discussion above about righteousness being a positive virtue for James rather than righteousness being the avoidance of particular sins. Then ask the question at the end of the lesson in the student book: ***"How do you seek to live according to God's will?"*** (*Most class members will likely say that they pray before making any major decision. Others will mention searching the Scriptures for guidance or getting the advice of a trusted Christian friend. Encourage interaction on this question; that is, have members ask one another follow-up questions to help all gain clarity on this crucial matter.*) Emphasize that, for James, living in keeping with God's will is nothing extraordinary. Rather, all of life is to be lived in an attitude of submission to God's will.

Bring this session to a conclusion with a prayer of confession, recalling past failures and resolving henceforth to follow Christ. You may want the group to pray together. Or you could have a silent prayer of confession, urging each person to lay his or her sins before God in silence. Then close with Charles Wesley's powerful and haunting hymn "A Charge to Keep I Have."

[1] From "The Baptismal Covenant II,"in *The United Methodist Hymnal* (Copyright © 1989 The United Methodist Publishing House); page 40.

TRY ANOTHER METHOD

■ If you have a room with tables to work on, a good way to express some ideas from this lesson would be to make collages. Form groups of three-to-five persons. Give each group a stack of old magazines, a pair of scissors, some paste, and a sheet of posterboard. Ask each group to make a collage illustrating James 4:1-2. If some groups have difficulty getting started, suggest that they look for illustrations of conflict and the causes of conflict. After eight-to-ten minutes, have the groups present their collages to the class.

Most of the collages will contain images of crime or warfare. As you view the collages, ask the class in regard to each: ***How do you see these conflicts as arising from "cravings that are at war within"?*** (*The members will probably identify motives such as greed, hatred, revenge, or lust behind their depictions of violence.*)

Then ask: ***How can we solve the problems we have seen presented?*** (*Many class members will question whether any real solution is possible. Others may propose solutions involving using superior force to shut down wars or to lock up criminals. Still others may suggest more positive solutions, based on education or aid.*)

Remind your class of James's assessment that conflicts and disputes derive from the kind of people that we are inside. The solution, for James, would lie in our becoming different people with different aims and motives. As James 4:7-10 reminds us, only through repentance and submission to God can we find our way to a new life.